# Teacher Take-Out 2

## for Grades one to six

### 12 Complete Lessons for Teachers on the Go!

Created by Becky Freeman

ISBN 0805402284

©1997 Broadman & Holman Supplies, Nashville, TN, printed in USA.

# Day 1: Let The Light Shine!

### (Based on Genesis 1:1-5)

Jake and Clint wound their way through the dark tunnels, with only the beam of a flashlight to guide them.

"Wow!" exclaimed Jake, "This is so cool. Why didn't you tell me about this cave before?"

Clint answered back over his shoulder. "Just discovered it last week when Dad and I were out camp—uh-oh." Suddenly everything around them went pitch black. "The flashlight's batteries had gone dead."

"Hey man—where are you?" It was Jake, and his voice had changed from excited to fearful.

"Don't worry," Clint said calmly, reaching into his pocket. "Dad warned me to always carry an extra set of batteries if I go exploring in caves. I've even got a little safety kit with matches and water and some food."

Within minutes the comforting light was shining through the darkness, leading the boys back out of the cave and into the daylight.

Jake rubbed his eyes, sat on a tree stump and said, "You know Clint, I never realized how much I loved the light until I was totally in the dark."

"I know what you mean," Clint answered with a grin. "I know what you mean."

—⁂—

When the earth began it had no shape at all. It was nothingness.

Empty. Dark.

God's Spirit was the only thing alive, hovering over the black waters. Then suddenly a voice thundered from God's Spirit and vibrated through the darkness. He said four little words.

"LET THERE BE LIGHT."

Even as the words were being spoken, like a flash of lightening, brilliant white light bathed the unformed earth. God liked what he saw, so He said, "Now that's good!"

Then He divided the light and the darkness into two parts. The darkness He called, "night" and the light He called, "day."

There was evening, then came morning. And that was the very first day, ever, on earth.

# Pin the Flame
## on the Candle
### *(Game for younger children)*

**Supplies:**
• blackboard or large sheet of butcher paper
• tape
• flames—cut out of yellow paper—one for each student
• crayons or marking pens
• bandanna or cloth for blindfold

Draw a big picture of a candle on the blackboard or a sheet of butcher paper taped to the wall. Give each child a piece of yellow paper cut into the shape of a flame. Have them write their name on the flame and stick a double-sided piece of tape on the back. Blindfold one child at a time and have them tape the flame where they think it might go on the candle. (Let the other children sing a chorus of "This Little Light of Mine" while the blindfolded child chooses where he'll put his flame.) After each child has his or her turn, remove their flame, holding your finger where they placed it, and write their name in the spot to mark it. Let the child who gets closest to the tip of the candle help hand out the papers for the next activity.

# Concordance Game
### *(Game for older children)*

**Supplies:**
• 2-3 New Testament concordances
• pens
• index cards or slips of paper

Begin by asking children, "What if you sort of remembered a verse, but you can't remember all of it and you don't know where it is in the Bible. How can you find it?"
After hearing some of their answers, show children how to look up words in a concordance in order to find the verses you are looking for in the Bible. Say, "Today we are going to divide into groups. I'll set the timer for 10 minutes. During that time your group is to look up all the verses it can find with the word "light" in it and write them out on index cards. Divide up the work and work as a team to help you get a lot of verses down quickly."

After the timer goes off, have each team count the verses they have. Team with most verses wins. Then have each team read at least one of the verses they've discovered about "light."

# Day 1: Let The Light Shine!
## Activity Sheet
### for Grades 1-3

Color the space around the candle on Figure A. Cut out candle picture on solid line. Fold in half on dashed line, then cut out candle. Open up and set it aside. Color the empty circle on Figure B a bright yellow. (Optional: spread it with a light covering of glue and sprinkle gold glitter on top.) Glue or tape Figure A on top of Figure B. Decorate the edges of Figure B with things that give off light, such as a sun, a lamp, matches, a fire, a flashlight, a light bulb, a lightning bug, lightning, and so on. Finish the sentence at the bottom with words from today's Bible story.

**Figure A**                    **Figure B**

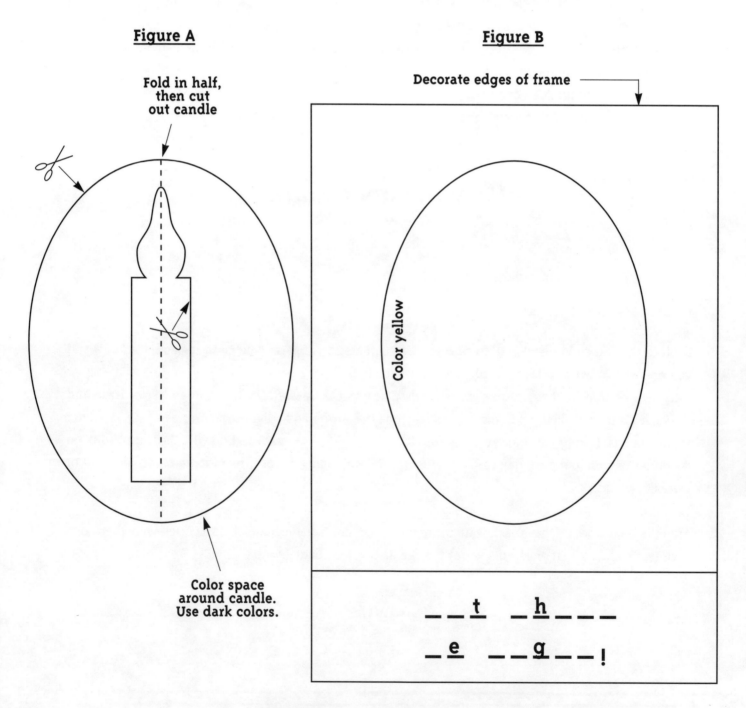

Fold in half,
then cut
out candle

Color space
around candle.
Use dark colors.

Decorate edges of frame

Color yellow

_ _ t  _ h _ _ _ _
_ e  _ _ g _ _ !

# Day 1: Let The Light Shine!

## Activity Sheet

### for Grades 4-6

Color all the spaces with one dot blue. Color the spaces with two dots green.
Color the spaces with three dots red. Color the spaces with four dots yellow.

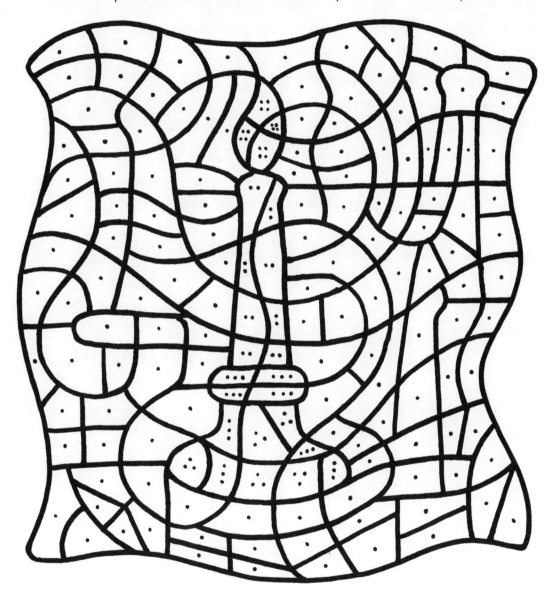

On the spaces below write "Let Your Light Shine" with 'invisible' white crayon printing.
Then, lay a dark-colored crayon on its side and color over the printing until it appears clearly.

_____

_____

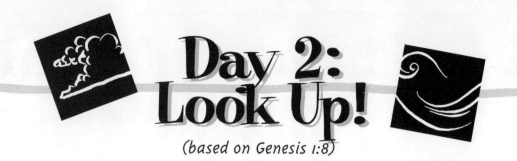

# Day 2: Look Up!

*(based on Genesis 1:8)*

Kate plopped down on the dock beside her friend, Shawn, letting her toes dangle in the lake water below. "Shawn," Kate said quietly, "I don't know if I really believe there's a God."

"WHAT?!" Shawn asked her best friend in surprise.

"Well, I mean, how do you know He is really real?"

"I just look up," answered Shawn matter-of-factly.

"Huh?"

"Look up there!" Shawn was pointing at the bright blue sky overhead. "Do you think that the sky, and that sun ball of fire, and those fluffy white clouds just appeared by themselves? What about the air that we breath? Who knew exactly what kind of gases would keep us alive and mixed them up just right? And what about the billions of stars and the galaxies we can't even see?"

"Okay, okay, okay!" shouted Kate.

"Okay what?" asked Shawn.

"Okay I see what you mean. Somebody had to create all this stuff and make it work together so perfectly. You're right. There has to be a Creator!"

Shawn smiled, and put her toes next to Kate's in the water. "So whenever you start to wonder if there's a God...."

Just then Kate laughed and splashed her feet in the water as she leaned her head back, and looking toward the heavens finished Shawn's thought. "I'll just look up!"

—◠◠◠—

After God made light to shine, He said something else. "Let there be a big space between the waters below and the waters above." Even as He spoke part of the waters began to rise up into the air and oceans of water stayed below. The filling between this "water sandwich" was a huge blue open space that God named, "sky."

Sky. That would be enough for today.

So evening came, then morning, and it was the second day of earth's creation. But it was the first day the earth sat under a brand new creation called, "Sky."

# Outdoor Sky Pictures

*(If it happens to be a pretty day, with fluffy clouds, and you can take the children outside)*

**Supplies:**
• white or manila paper
• pencils
• a quilt

Give every child some white paper and a pencil. Bring a quilt outside and instruct the children to get comfortable on the quilt, then to draw everything that they see in the sky on their paper. It's also fun to see if together, you and the class can see shapes that look like animals or other things in the cloud formations.

# Indoor Sky Murals

*(If it is best to stay indoors)*

**Supplies:**
• Five to eight feet of butcher paper
• markers
• construction paper
• scraps
• scissors
• pencils
• tape or glue sticks

Across the top of a large sheet of white or light blue butcher paper, write the verse from Genesis 1:8 that says, "God called the expanse 'sky.'" You may hang the paper on the wall or lay it on a large table, covering it like a table cloth. (You may want to tape down the edges if they try to curl up.) Then give the children scraps of construction paper, pencils and scissors and let them fill the blank sky with anything they can think of that goes up, stays or comes down from the sky: balloons, clouds, birds, planes, rainbow, raindrops, snow flakes, etc. Don't forget angels and even a picture of Jesus as they think He might look coming back in the clouds someday.

# God Made The Sky
*(sing to the tune of Amazing Grace)*

Read Psalm 103: 11 out loud to the class, then sing the following song together.

*God made the sky for all to see*
*His love, so high, for me*
*He sends the clouds, the rain and the sun*
*The stars when day is done*

# Day 2: Look Up!
## Activity Sheet
### for Grades 1-3

Would you like to fly in your very own hot air balloon? Pretend this is your balloon and decorate it the way you'd want a real hot air balloon to look if you had one. Then draw yourself in the basket. Show all the things you'd love to see from up high in the sky around you and below. Write the words, "God made the sky!" in the four clouds.

# Day 2: Look Up!
## Activity Sheet
### for Grades 4-6

Fill in the crossword puzzle with things that appear in the sky. Look up the verses to help you find clues.
You may want to do this as a whole class and take turns reading the verses out loud.
(Note: Most verses are found in the book of Psalms or the book of Matthew.)

**Across**
1. Genesis 9:13
2. Matthew 18:19
3. Psalm 136:9
4. Psalm 50:1
5. Psalm 104: 19

**Down**
1. Matthew 13:32
2. Psalm 103:5
3. Matthew 24:30
4. Matthew 8:27
5. Genesis 7:12

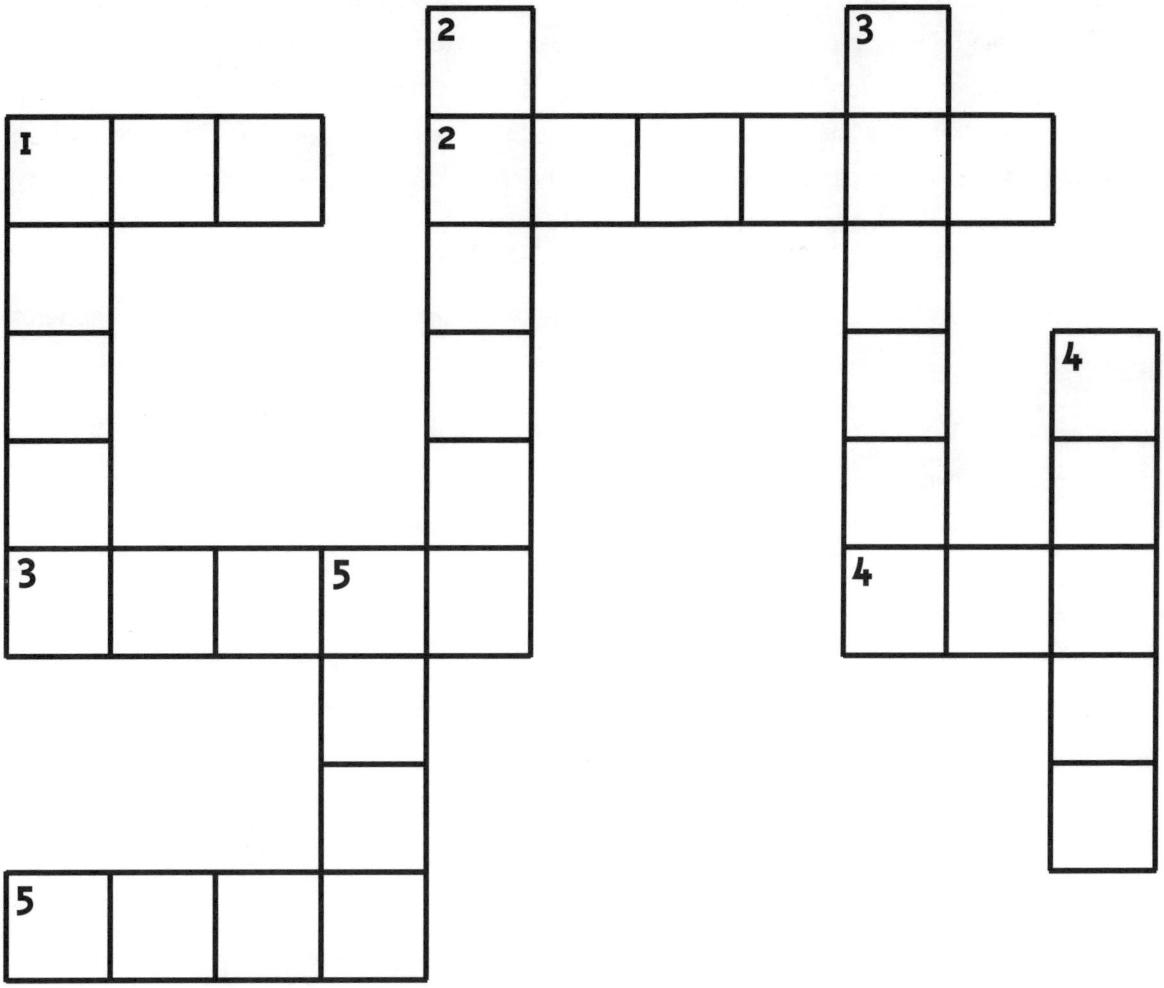

# Day 3: Growing Good Stuff!

*(based on Genesis 1:9-13)*

Lindsay pulled up a stool to the kitchen counter to get a better view of what her Mother was up to. "Whatcha doin' Mom?" she asked as she propped her chin in the cup of her hands.

"I'm making some healthy snacks for tomorrow's party at work," Mrs. Bigby explained. Lindsay loved to visit her mom at work. Who wouldn't? Her mother worked part-time as a nutritionist at the local zoo. She knew exactly what to feed every animal from the baby orangutan (Lindsay's favorite) to the tallest giraffe.

Mrs. Bigby took a big knife and cut a chunk out of the center of a watermelon. Then, with a few simple strokes, she carved the watermelon into the shape of a whale!

"That looks great, Mom!" Lindsay exclaimed.

Thanks, honey. Now watch this!? Taking the sharp knife, Mrs. Bigby cut a fresh yellow pear in half, lengthwise—scooped out the seeds and laid one half, flat side down, on a plate of lettuce leaves. Then she squirted a dollop of whipped cream near the fat end of the pear, to make a fluffy tail. On the narrow end of the pear, she placed a tiny piece of cherry for a nose, then stuck in two slices of almond for ears.

Lindsay squealed, "It's a bunny in the grass! It's so cute! I don't think anyone should ever eat it."

"I'm glad you like it. I thought it would be fun to make the food look like animals since it's a zoo party. Now for the veggie tray...."? Mrs. Bigby bent to pull a bag of fresh carrots, broccoli and celery from the crisper, then looked up at her daughter and said, "Isn't God creative to give us, and the animals, too, all these great fruits and vegetables to eat? They not only feed our bodies, but our eyes! Just look at these bright colors!"

Lindsay nodded enthusiastically, opened her mouth and took a big bite of juicy, red watermelon.

—⚹—

Everywhere there was water, water, and still more water. Until God said, "Let the water gather up in one place and let dry land appear." With those words, oceans of water moved over and huge pieces of ground appeared from nowhere to decorate the earth. God called the water "seas" and the dry ground He named "land." God very much liked what He saw happening. But there was still more to come.

The voice boomed out across the sea and land. "Let the land be covered with plants and trees that bear fruit. Let them have seeds inside so that when the fruit and plants drop to the ground, more will grow in its place."

God saw bright green leaves and vines spring up and cover the earth with color. Then hundreds of different kinds of flowers and fruits and vegetables appeared. What a colorful sight!

The earth was now three days old—and growing more beautiful everyday.

# Growing Food

**Supplies:**
- Alfalfa seeds or other fast sprouting seeds from the health food store, poured into a large plastic bowl
- Several spoons
- Pitcher of water
- Small canning jars with rings and lids removed
- Clean nylon hose cut up into squares, or other fine mesh

Tell children that they are going to get to grow their own food this week. Give each child a clean jar and instruct them to put about a tablespoon of seeds into their jar. Then have them cover the seeds with water and swish seeds around until they are all rinsed and wet. Next, cover the mouth of the jar with a piece of nylon hose or mesh.

Place the metal ring over the material and screw onto jar. Then have the children drain the water out of their jars (mesh will keep seeds from spilling out) into a sink or another empty bowl. Write names on their jars with permanent marker or onto a piece of masking tape. Tell them, "Rinse your seeds every day and set the jar in a sunny window. In about 3 or 4 days you should see that the seeds have turned into tiny plants called sprouts.

Put the sprouts on your peanut butter sandwich or in a salad or eat them plain. Mmmm, good!"

# Sea, Land, Plants Game

**Supplies:**
- paper
- pin
- poster or chalkboard as a reference for game rules

Put the following information on the chalkboard or a poster:

Plants cover the land

Land covers the sea

Sea covers the plants (when it turns to rain)

Five fingers up = plants

Hand down flat = land

Hand in a fist = sea

Tell the children, "This is played just like the old 'Paper, Rock, Scissors' game but since we read about how God created 'Sea, Land, and Plants' we are using those instead."

Help children divide into pairs. Demonstrate how the game is played. On the count of three the pair of players must both at the same time show their "hand." Using the chart above find out who wins the round. For example, since "plants cover the land" the child with five fingers up (plants) wins over the child with flat hand down (land). Have children keep their score on a piece of paper. Once they get the idea, you can let the children play this on their own with very little supervision. Decide in advance how long you will let them play. A timer helps. Let the winners stand up and take a bow!

# Day 3: Growing Good Stuff!
## Activity Sheet
### for Grades 1-3

Fill in your favorite growing things on each of the petals as indicated. Also draw and color a picture of your favorite thing on each petal. Color the center of the flower. Then cut out the petals and the flower's middle and glue the pieces together on a piece of construction paper, using glue sticks. Teacher may want to bring books with pictures and names of a variety of plants, flowers, vegetables, fruits, and trees to help.

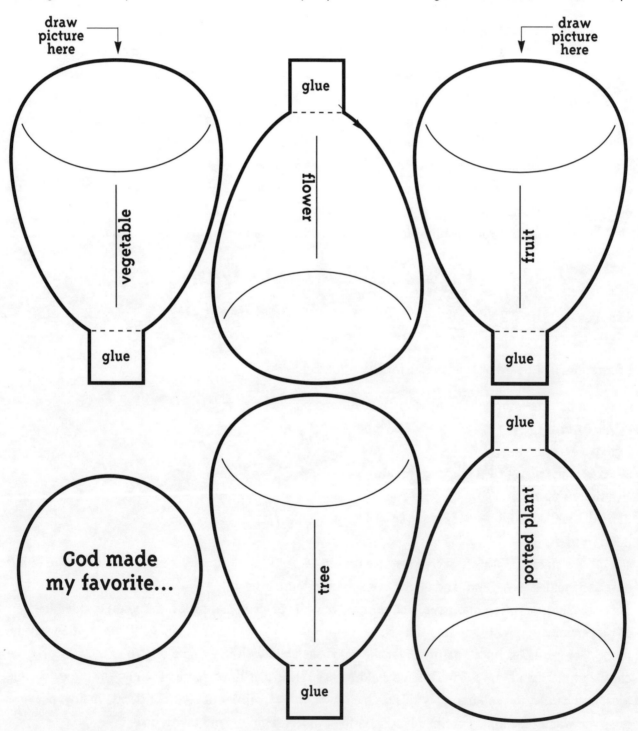

draw picture here

vegetable

glue

flower

glue

draw picture here

fruit

glue

God made my favorite...

tree

glue

glue

potted plant

# Day 3: Growing Good Stuff!
## Activity Sheet
### for Grades 4-6

Unscramble the names of fruits and vegetables below.
Then decorate the fruit basket and vegetable tray with pictures of those fruits and vegetables.

**Fruit Basket**          **Veggie Tray**

**Fruit Basket**

1. plapse    _ _ _ _ _ _
2. iikw    _ _ _ _
3. onamg    _ _ _ _ _
4. arsewrtbseir    _ _ _ _ _ _ _ _ _ _ _ _
5. ntaocpelau    _ _ _ _ _ _ _ _ _ _

**Veggie Tray**

1. ronc    _ _ _ _
2. lcobiroc    _ _ _ _ _ _ _ _
3. yclree    _ _ _ _ _ _
4. srsuaagpa    _ _ _ _ _ _ _ _ _
5. trorcsa    _ _ _ _ _ _ _
6. harsdi    _ _ _ _ _ _

©1997 Broadman & Holman, Teacher Take-Out 2, Grades 1-6

# Day 4: Seasons of Light

*(based on Genesis 1:14-19)*

Joey and his dad lay in lawn chairs on the back porch, looking up at the sky. Night had fallen several minutes ago. Now they were just waiting. "When will it be?" Joey asked impatiently.

"Wait and see," Dad said, "wait and see."

Just then Joey thought he saw something shoot across the sky. It was a streak of light that went by so fast he almost missed it. "Was that a...?"

"Yes, it was."

"A real shooting star?" Joey wanted to make sure.

"Yes, Son and—look! There goes another one!"

Joey was glad that his dad let him stay up to watch stars. Sometimes his dad even took him on after-dark "moon walks," when the moon was fat and round.

"Dad, if it weren't for the sun it would be dark all the time wouldn't it?"

"Yes, and so cold that I'm afraid nothing could grow. We couldn't even live without the sun."

"And if it weren't for the moon and stars, there'd be no lights at all in the night?"

"That's right, only pitch black darkness."

"I think it's awfully nice of God to give us lights in the day and in the nighttime, don't you?"

"Yes, son. And remember that even if you go through sad, lonely, dark times in life God will always be there shining like a star in the night reminding you of His love."

"Dad?"

"Yes, son?"

"I love you."

"I love you, too, Joey. I love you, too."

—⁓—

God liked light so much that he put lights in the sky both day and night. The biggest light was the sun. The smaller one, the moon. Then he sprinkled the dark velvet night with diamonds of stars just for man to look at and wonder about. "The lights will be good signs to help mark seasons and days and years," God said.

Another evening but this time the moon and stars shone above.

Another morning, but this morning the sun rose over the horizon and when it set in the western sky it brushed the sky with new colors of orange and purple and glowing red.

The earth was four days old.

When God made the moon and the sun, He set the seasons into motion, too. The following is a rhyming play for the whole class. Make copies to hand out to your students or enlarge and put on an overhead or large flip chart. After practicing it once, try to have fun with it by speaking it with a rap or jazz beat or making up a snappy tune. Then, add hand motions.

**All:** Fall is my fav-o-rite season (hands up, fingers wriggling like leaves on an autumn tree)

**Speaker #1:** September, October, November

**All:** Fall is my favorite season (repeat hand motion)

**Speaker #2:** Thanksgiving is what I remember!

**All:** Spring is my favorite season (bring arms up, like plants growing to the sun)

**Speaker #3:** March, April, and May

**All:** Spring is my favorite season

**Speaker #4:** Jesus rose on Easter Day

**All:** Winter is my favorite season (hug yourself as if trying to get warm)

**Speaker #5:** December, January, February

**All:** Winter is my favorite season

**Speaker #6:** Jesus Birthday makes it so merry

**All:** Summer is my favorite season (put hands up as if to shade eyes from sun)

**Speaker #7:** June, July, and August

**All:** Summer is my favorite season

**Speaker #8:** Come in and take a swim with us!

**All:** Seasons are all so very special (both arms open wide)

**Speaker #9:** Winter, Spring, Summer, and Fall

**All:** Seasons are all so very special

**Speaker #10:** I guess I'll have to love them all!

# Day 4: Seasons of Light
## Activity Sheet
### for Grade 1-3

Using what you learned in today's Bible story, fill in all the missing letters with a dark pen, then lightly color each source of light. Cut out stars, moon and sun and the rectangular block. (You may want to glue worksheet to construction paper for added strength before cutting out.) Hang lights from the rectangle with string or strips of paper to make a mobile.

God made two great lights — one for the d _ _ and one for n _ _ _ _ . He also made s _ _ _ _ .

_ _ A _

H _ _ _ _
M _ _ _ _

F _ _ L
_ _ O _

_ _ _ R

S _ _

# Day 4: Seasons of Light
## Activity Sheet
### for Grades 4-6

God gave us the moon and sun as signs of the seasons.
Follow the instructions to decorate your calendar of months and seasons:
Some months will have more than one picture.

1. Draw a birthday cake in your birthday month.
2. Draw a manger in the month that we celebrate Jesus' birth.
3. Draw an angel at an open tomb in one of the months we celebrate Easter (it changes from year to year).
4. Draw an umbrella and raindrops in the month that brings lots of showers.
5. Draw a kite in the springtime month that starts with an "m" and has five letters.
6. Draw a sun in the last month of the summer.
7. Draw an apple and a pencil in the first whole month you are in school.
8. Draw a pumpkin in the month before the Thanksgiving month.
9. Draw praying hands in the month we celebrate Thanksgiving.
10. Draw a flag in the month America celebrates Independence Day.
11. Draw a beach ball in the first month of summer.
12. Draw a heart in the month where we celebrate Valentine's Day.
13. Draw a snowman in the month after Christmas.
14. Draw a flower in the month after April showers.

Copy Genesis 1:14 in the blank at the top of the calendar.

---

**Genesis 1:14**

| December | January | February |
| --- | --- | --- |
| March | April | May |
| June | July | August |
| September | October | November |

# Day 5: Of Feathers and Fins

*(from Genesis 1:20-23)*

Mandy and her brother, Blake, burst through the door of the pet store holding their money tight in their hands. They were twins and yesterday was their birthday. Finally, Mom and Dad had said they could each pick out a pet.

"But it has to be small," said Mom.

"And not much trouble," added Dad.

"And," they both said, "it can't run around our small apartment. Oh, look!" Mandy and Blake said at the same time, as they walked towards pets at different ends of the store. Mandy stood on her tip-toes and peered into several birdcages. There were two cooing love birds and lots of pretty yellow canaries. The finches were adorable so tiny and sweet. "How did God think of so many different kinds? And how will I ever choose just one?" she thought. Then a green parakeet caught Mandy's eye.

"Hello," she said.

"Hel-lo! Hel-lo!" he sang right back.

Mandy laughed. She had made her choice.

Over in the corner of the store, Blake stood with his nose pressed against the giant aquarium. He especially loved watching the tropical fish, their colors so bright it was hard to believe they were real. Bright blue, neon greens, lemon yellows, brilliant orange. Finally he settled on a perfect black and yellow angel fish.

The twins left the store with huge smiles on their faces. Blake had a pet with fins and Mandy, a pet with feathers.

"Well, Blake," said Mandy, "I wonder what Mom and Dad will say when we walk in the door?"

But before Blake could speak, the parakeet answered by saying, "Hel-lo, Hel-lo, Hel-lo!"

And he was right. As soon as the twins walked through the front door, that's exactly what Mom and Dad said.

—⁓—

Now the background was set. There was food and water and land and air to breathe. Time to create something special. God spoke, "Let the waters fill up with living creatures."

And the oceans filled with giant whales with their spouts spewing water, and trillions of microscopic sea creatures. In a moment, thousands of fish and sea animals of every variety began to dive and swish and swim through the waves. God delighted in what He had created. The dark, quiet waters were gone, now His ocean was bursting with life.

Then He spoke the word and the sky came alive too. Sparrows and eagles and ducks and geese, all soaring and swooping with joy on their wings. God not only saw that this was good, He blessed his new creatures.

"Swim! Fly! Live! And have lots and lots of babies until the sea and sky is running over with your kind!"

The fifth day on Earth was a noisy one. And a very, very happy one.

# The Fishing Puzzle Game

**Supplies:**
- paper
- magnets
- paper clips
- string
- a 2½ inch stick
- books or magazines with pictures of birds and fish
- crayons
- pencils

Before class starts, draw a big simple fish shape (about a foot to a foot and a half square). Sketch some simple scales, an eye and the words "God made fish" on it with a marker. Then cut the fish into puzzle shapes. (NOTE: For grades 1-3, keep the puzzle shapes big. For grades 4-6, cut them smaller and make the puzzle more challenging. Turn the pieces of the puzzle face down on the floor attaching a paper clip to each piece. Don't let the children know what the puzzle will make.

Make a fishing pole with a stick, a string, and a good magnet tied onto the end as a hook. Let one child at a time go fishing. When he or she gets her catch have them take their piece to a table and try to help put the puzzle together. You may extend this activity by doing the same thing with a simple shape of a bird.

While waiting for turns, another table may be set up with books on fish and birds, pencil, paper and colors or markers. Encourage the children to try to sketch their favorite fish or bird that they find in the book. Allow time for them to share their art and to talk about the fascinating life God created under the sea and in the air.

# Day 5: Of Feathers and Fins
## Activity Sheet
### for Grades 1-3

Color the scenes below and the fish and birds on the right. Cut the scene in half along the dotted line to make two pictures. Carefully make slits in the nest and in the water. Cut out the baby birds and slide them in the nest. Cut out the momma bird and glue just her middle to the sky. Draw a worm in her beak. Fold her wings up to give it a two dimensional look. Slide fish into slits on the lake. You can make the baby birds go up and down as they wait for momma bird to bring the worm; or make the fish jump out of the water.

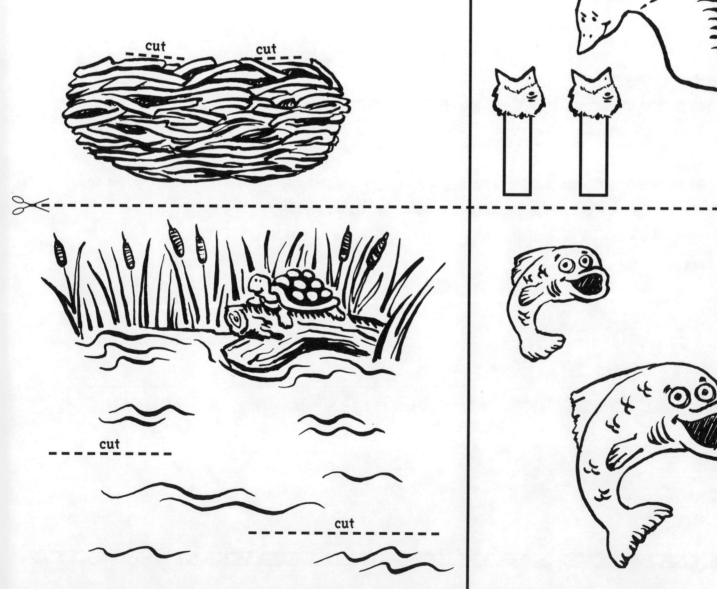

fold up
wings

cut        cut

cut

cut

cut

# Day 5: Of Feathers and Fins
## Activity Sheet
### for Grades 4-6

Try to answer (or guess) at the following questions without having to look up the verse.
Then check your answers and see if you were right.

**Famous Fish Facts**

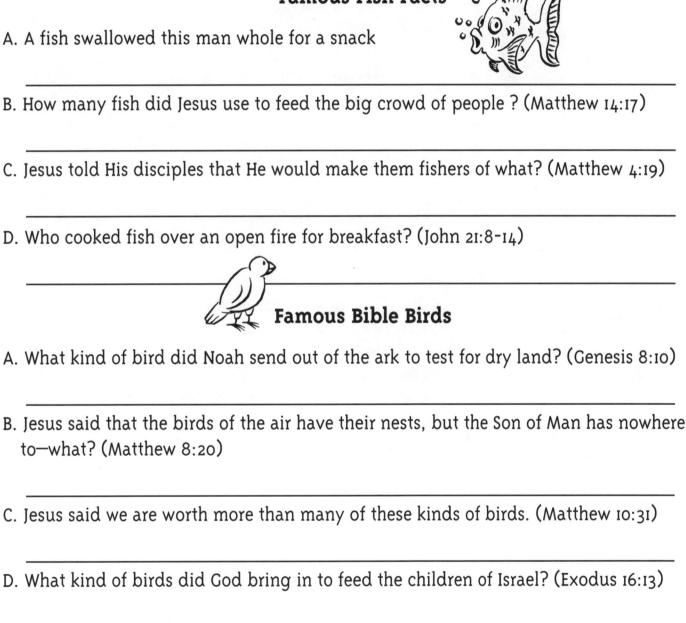

A. A fish swallowed this man whole for a snack

_____

B. How many fish did Jesus use to feed the big crowd of people ? (Matthew 14:17)

_____

C. Jesus told His disciples that He would make them fishers of what? (Matthew 4:19)

_____

D. Who cooked fish over an open fire for breakfast? (John 21:8-14)

_____

**Famous Bible Birds**

A. What kind of bird did Noah send out of the ark to test for dry land? (Genesis 8:10)

_____

B. Jesus said that the birds of the air have their nests, but the Son of Man has nowhere to—what? (Matthew 8:20)

_____

C. Jesus said we are worth more than many of these kinds of birds. (Matthew 10:31)

_____

D. What kind of birds did God bring in to feed the children of Israel? (Exodus 16:13)

_____

E. Jesus was once very sad because the people would not listen to Him, even though He would have gathered them like—what? (Matthew 23:37)

_____

# Day 6: God Made the Animals
## —Even Snakes, Bugs and Frogs!

*(From Genesis 1:24-25)*

"Wait till you see this!"

"See what?" asked Alicia.

"Look over on that rock there!" Her brother, Nathan was pointing to a big rock.

Alicia wanted to scream but she was too afraid to make a noise. A huge snake was sunning himself on the rock. Nathan whispered, "It's poisonous, so don't touch it."

"Don't worry," Alicia whispered back.

"He's beautiful," said Nathan.

Alicia wondered about her big brother sometimes. Suddenly she felt something tickling the back of her neck.

Nathan yelled, "Don't move! There's a fantastic spider on your hair. "He's perfect for my collection!"

Alicia could feel her heart beating wildly and wondered how hard she would land if she fainted right now.

Nathan held the spider in the palm of his hand, stroking it and talking to it as if it were a baby. Alicia shook her head and sat down on a stump.

"God makes the most wonderful creatures," Nathan was saying aloud as he looked under logs in search of interesting insects. Alicia was feeling a little sick to her stomach so she slid on down to the ground and lay there looking up at the sky, hoping she'd soon feel better.

"Alicia where are you?" Nathan asked, looking around.

"Down here," she said from her resting spot on the ground before Nathan almost stepped on her.

"What are you doing down th —?" but Nathan didn't get to finish his sentence. For at that moment a giant green bullfrog leaped out of the nearby stream and landed—splat—on his sister's forehead. Nathan was thrilled: it was just the sort of frog he'd been hoping to find.

—⁂—

Now that the sea and the sky were getting filled up, God was ready to liven up the land. So He made cows and critters and creeping things. All sorts of wild beasts: from boars to baboons. Lizards and frogs and polliwogs. Horses and cats and rhinos and dogs and on and on and on.

Last of all, he made a man and a woman. He made them last because He loved them most—and wanted to give them a world full of wonders to explore. Like a sky full of birds and a sea filled with fish.

The sun, moon and stars. Mountains and caves. Good food to eat. And enough animals to keep them laughing for a long, long time.

# Play Animal Charades

Divide the class into two parts. Take turns letting each team send someone up to act out an animal (without making any noises). They can only take one minute and then the next team gets to try. Team who guesses the most animals correctly within the time limit wins. (You may want to let them be the first to be served some animal crackers.)

Here's a list to get you started:

**Bee**

**Elephant**

**Monkey**

**Rabbit**

**Giraffe**

**Horse**

**Dog**

**Cat**

**Beaver**

**Frog**

**Mouse**

**Snake**

# Animal Alphabet

Another game is to go around the room and let each person think of an animal to go with a letter of the alphabet. For example, player number one might say, "A -Aardvark." Player number two, "B-Baboon." And so on until you have gone through the entire alphabet. (It's okay to skip over the letter "x.")

# Day 6: God Made the Animals
## —Even Snakes, Bugs and Frogs!
### Activity Sheet
#### for Grades 1-3

Color and cut out the animal cards below. Turn them face down and mix them up. Then turn them over two at a time trying to find a matching pair. (Alternate game: Choose a partner. Turn cards face down as before. Player 1 turns over 2 cards. If they match, Player 1 keeps the matching cards and turns over 2 more cards. Player 1 continues until 2 cards do not match. Then Player 2 gets a turn. Players go back and forth until all cards have been matched. Player with most matches at the end, wins.)

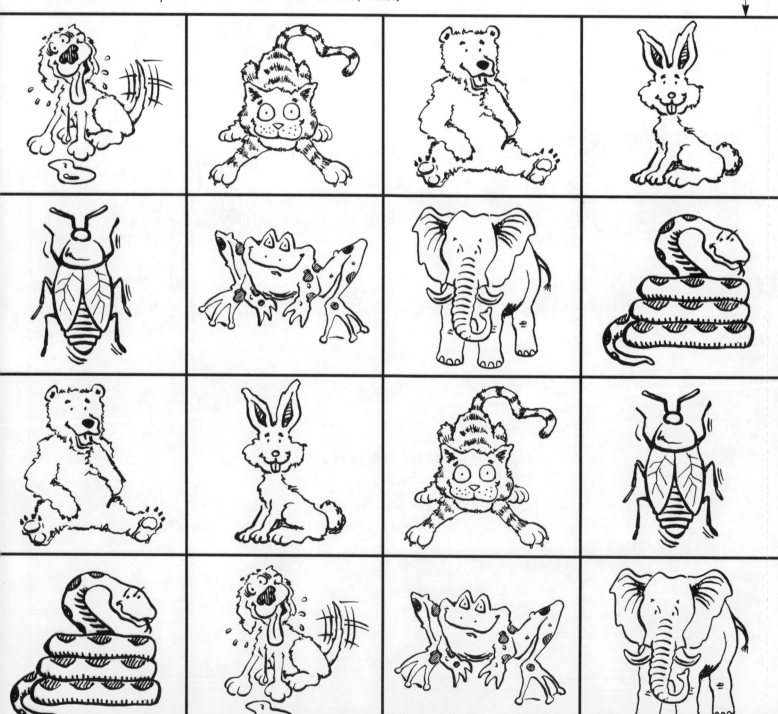

# Day 6: God Made the Animals
## —Even Snakes, Bugs and Frogs!
### Activity Sheet
**for Grades 4-6**

Decorate the snake with a design that follows a pattern. Cut alone the spiral line.
Color tongue red and glue or tape to snake's mouth. Color strips green.
Follow pictured instructions to make a frog. Use tape to attach ends.

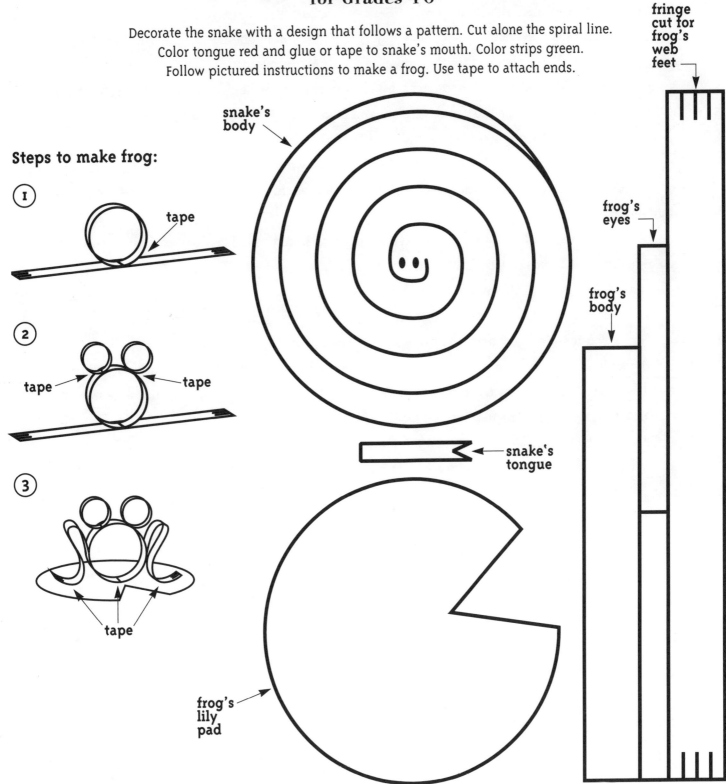

**Steps to make frog:**

1 — tape

2 — tape — tape

3 — tape

snake's body

snake's tongue

fringe cut for frog's web feet

frog's eyes

frog's body

frog's lily pad

# Day 7: God Took Time for Rest

*(Genesis 2:2-3)*

then & now

"Lisa!" Mom's voice echoed down the hall, "Have you cleaned your room yet?"

Lisa sat up on her bed feeling groggy and angry. "NO! And I'm not going to either. I'm tired of you always being on my back about getting my room clean. It's MY room any...."

Before Lisa could finish her sentence, her mother's presence made her suddenly sorry she'd opened her mouth. Mother had one eyebrow raised and a hand on one hip. This was not a good sign.

"I'm sorry, Mom," Lisa confessed sincerely.

"What's the matter with you?" her Mother asked, her brow wrinkled in worry.

"I'm just so tired I don't even know what I'm saying. I stayed up all night at Kay's slumber party last night and my head is all muddled."

"Ah," Mother responded, the warmth slowly creeping back into her voice. "I never understood why you girls call those things slumber parties. Nobody ever sleeps or slumbers."

"I know. They're so much fun, but the next day ...."

"Lisa, part of being a human being is we have to rest and recharge in order to work right."

"I know you're right Mo-o-om," Lisa said as she yawned.

"Think about this," her mother continued, "even God took six days to create the earth and took the seventh off to rest. I think He was setting an example for us: to work best we need to do our work in small daily chunks and then take regular time off just to sleep and relax."

"Okaaay. Do I have to clean my room right now or can I take a nap first?"

"Tell you what. I'll let you sleep for a couple of hours and then get started on your room. This time. But from now on, you need to either get your room clean before you go off to a slumber party or tell the girls you've GOT to go to bed at a decent time. Deal?"

"Deal!" Lisa's head hit the pillow and she was snoring by the time her mother tip-toed out the door.

—⚏—

A job well done. God had finished the work he had been doing on the earth, so He took time to rest and enjoy it. He even blessed the day and called it "holy." He knew we would also need rest times, times to pause and say "thank you" for all of His goodness. That's why, all over the world, families take a break from work and spend part of Sunday worshiping God. He's our Creator and He knows how we work best.

# Bedtime Memory Game

**Supplies:**

In a big clean trash bag gather about 10 items that remind us of bedtime or sleep. Examples are: a small pillow, blanket, tooth brush, a mug, graham crackers, a book, a pair of pajamas, Teddy Bear or other stuffed animal, alarm clock, night light, flash light, diary or notebook, Bible, some concrete symbol of prayer (a figurine, praying hands, a picture of someone praying, etc.). Put on a cassette or CD of lullabies or soft music so the children will begin to unwind as they come into the room. You might even let them gather on the floor on a quilt and use the soft light of a lamp instead of the regular room lighting. Also, gather any Christian picture books that seem to be of a relaxing nature.

Show the children all the things you brought in the sack and spread them out on the floor or table so everyone can see. Tell them you are going to give them a minute to look and then put all the items back in the trashbag. That's when they'll see how many items they can remember. Older children should write down the names of the items on a card or a piece of paper, individually. Younger ones may prefer to draw pictures instead of writing the words, or you may do this as a group project with them. If you'd like, you may want to serve a snack of graham crackers and milk or juice as a mid-morning "bedtime" snack. With any time left over, gather the children around and read from a couple of children's books.

# Day 7: God Took Time for Rest

## Activity Sheet

### for Grades 1-3

Write name on the pillow beside the nighty-night quilt.
Then color your quilt and decorate the blank squares by doing the following:

Square #1   Draw a favorite stuffed animal.

Square #2   Draw your favorite bedtime snack.

Square #3   Draw the cover of your favorite book.

Square #4   Draw what you think your guardian angel may look like.

Square #5   Draw praying hands.

Square #6   Draw any design you like.

Square #7   Draw a picture of the moon.

Square #8   Draw some stars.

(Teacher: you may need to do this as a class for beginning readers)

# Day 7: God Took Time for Rest
## Activity Sheet
### for Grades 4-6

## Bible Sleepytimes

Match the following names with the description of what
happened when this person (or those around him) fell asleep.
Scriptures are listed for those that may be tricky.

1. Jesus, as a grown man

2. Joseph, Mary's husband
   (Matthew. 2:19)

3. Jacob
   (Matthew. 2:19)

4. Adam

5. Jesus, as a baby

6. Disciples

7. Samson

8. Samuel
   (1 Samuel 3:8)

9. Moses, as a baby

10. David

A. Got his haircut and his strength zapped

B. Slept in a box that holds animal's food

C. Fell asleep in the boat in the middle of a storm
   (Jonah 1:5)

D. Slept in a basket floating in the water

E. Sang to his sheep at night

F. Lost a rib, got a wife

G. Had a dream about escaping to Egypt

H. Dreamed of a ladder reaching to heaven

I. Heard God calling him at night — 3 times

J. Fell asleep while Jesus prayed in a garden

# A Long Journey
## (based on Luke 2:1-5)

Robert pushed his glasses back where they belonged by wrinkling up his nose. He was already having one of the hardest days of his life and it wasn't even noon yet! "I hate being the new kid in school," he thought as he struggled not to let any tears slip out. "I miss my old friends."

Now it was lunch time and Robert carried his tray of spaghetti and salad over to the lunch table and looked for a spot to sit down. No such luck.

"Sorry, this seat's saved."

"Dustin always sits by me."

"Why don't you go sit down at the end of the table by the teacher?"

By the time Robert found a place to sit down, he wasn't hungry anymore. At recess, Robert wandered around the edge of the field, wishing he were anywhere else but at this new school where he had no friends. Just then, a kid with freckles across his nose, wearing a baseball hat on backwards said, "Hey, my name's Skeet, you wanna play catch? I've got a glove and I know where we can get a ball."

For the first time all day, the knot in Robert's stomach stopped hurting. He had to admit, Skeet was a nice kid. And funny. He kept calling Robert "New Guy" but it was a friendly sort of teasing. Robert even kind of liked the nickname. Finally, the school bell rang and Robert walked up the steps to the bus.

"Sorry, this seat's saved," he heard someone say as he walked by. Oh, no not again. But there was something familiar about that voice. He looked down and saw Skeet laughing and patting the seat next to him.

"I saved it for YOU, New Guy."

Finally, a place to rest and belong.

—⁓—

With each step Mary felt the baby within her grow heavier. The pains were coming hard now and fast. "Joseeeph!" she cried as she squeezed his hand.

"Mary, I've checked every room in the city. There's not one room available!"

"Oh, Joseph, I can't have this child on the streets of Bethlehem."

"Don't worry, Mary, God gave you this child. He'll find us a place."

To Joseph's surprise, the place God found for His Son to be born was in a stall for ANIMALS! Mary didn't mind the straw and the cows. She only wanted to gaze into the eyes of her newborn child. It was simply good to be quiet and have a place to rest. Even if her bed was hay and her child was sleeping in a manger.

# True or False

**Supplies:**
- paper plates
- crayons
- optional: tape and popsicle sticks

Give every child a paper plate and instruct them to write the word "true" on one side and "false" on the other. To make a fancier sign, they may tape the plate to a popsicle stick, but it's not necessary. Read the following statements from today's scriptures and tell the children to hold the side for "true" facing the teacher if they agree with the sentence and "false" if they disagree. If you've not read the Scripture, it is a good idea to read the passage aloud right now, letting them know they'll be quizzed on it. (Luke 2: 1-5)

1. Joseph and Mary went to Nazareth to pay taxes (F)

2. Mary wrapped Jesus in fur and laid him in a manger (F)

3. Mary's baby was born in a stable (T)

4. Joseph spent the night in the inn while Mary slept in the barn (F)

5. Bethlehem is also called the Town of George (F)

6. Jesus was Mary's first child (T)

7. Caesar Salad was the ruler of the Roman World (F)

8. Nazareth is in Galilee (T)

9. Bethlehem is in Judea (T)

10. Jesus was born in Nazareth (F)

11. Jesus grew up in Bethlehem (F)

12. There was no room in the inn because they were remodeling the rooms (F)

13. Mary wrapped Jesus in cloths and put him in danger (F)

14. Mary wrapped Jesus in cloths and put him in a manger (T)

15. A manger is a nice baby bed with mattress and box springs attached (F)

16. A manger is where cows eat their hay (T)

17. Mary and Joseph had lots of money (F)

18. Mary and Joseph loved and followed God (T)

# A Long Journey
## Activity Sheet
### for Grades 1-3

Color the picture below. Then cut along the solid lines. Don't cut on any dashed lines.
You may want to use this as a Christmas card or decoration.

**Example**

✂ - - - - - - - - - - - - - - - - - - - - - - - - - - - - - - - - - - - - - - - - - -

**Fold under**
- - - - - - - - - - - - - - - - - - - - - - - - - - - - - - - - - - - - - - - - - - - - - -

Fold

Fold

## Is there room in your heart for Him?

**Fold under**

# A Long Journey
## Activity Sheet
### for Grades 4-6

1. The map below shows the places where Jesus lived and taught and died. The dot farthest North is Nazareth, the hometown of Mary and Joseph, where Jesus grew up. Put the name "Nazareth" by the correct dot.

2. The dot farthest south is Bethlehem, the city of Jesus birth. Label that dot.

3. The dot just above Bethlehem is Jerusalem where Jesus often visited the temple. Write "Jerusalem" on that dot.

4. Joseph and Mary had to travel all the way from Nazareth to Bethlehem to register for taxes. Draw a red line on the map below to show their journey.

5. It was 70 miles between Nazareth and Bethlehem. How long do you think it took Mary and Joseph to travel that distance by foot? _____

6. See the little kidney bean shaped lake in Galilee? That is actually The Sea of Galilee where Jesus often loved to teach. Label that and color it blue.

7. The larger body of water is called The Dead Sea. Label that and color it blue.

8. The stripe between the Sea of Galilee and the Dead Sea is called The Jordan River, where Jesus was baptized. Label it and go over the line with blue.

9. Color the Mediterranean Sea blue, and the land brown or green

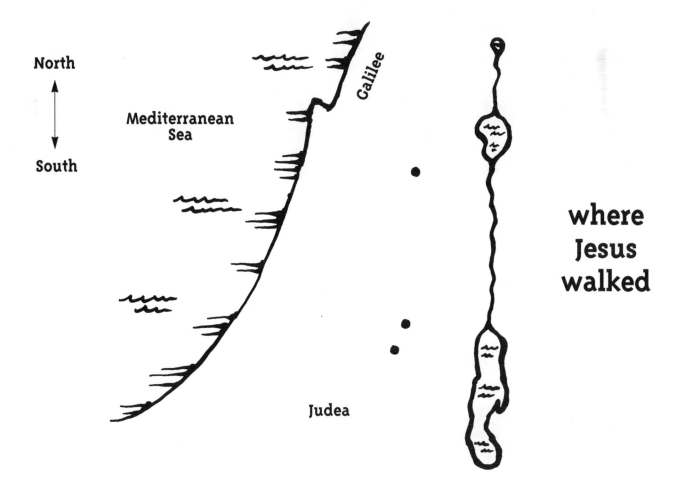

North

Mediterranean
Sea

South

Galilee

where
Jesus
walked

Judea

# Thank You for Coming!

*(Luke 2:6-7)*

Charissa Long had been waiting all morning for this. She sat on the front porch watching every car that passed, thinking it might be the one that held the treasure. Finally, the familiar blue sedan pulled up to the curb. In a flash, Charissa was at the open car door, with her arms outstretched. Just inside the front seat, Charissa's mother looked tired, but happy. She gently handed Charissa the bundle wrapped in powder blue. Charissa lifted the corner of the blanket and stared into the sweetest little face she'd ever seen. This would be the best Christmas ever.

"Hello, Baby Brother," she said tenderly. Then she looked at her mother and said, "I've been praying we'd get one of these for years!"

Mrs. Long laughed as her husband helped her , gently, out of the car. Mr. Long gave his daughter a wink and with his Texas accent said, "Well, Sweetheart, you prayed good!"

Later as Charissa rocked her new brother, she held his little toes and fingers and was amazed at how tiny and perfect he was. She thought of the soft bed and blankets of blue that lined his bassinet. She looked over at the nativity scene on the fireplace mantel, and thought about baby Jesus. He had also been tiny, and delicate. But he was born in a stable? Put to bed in a manger of hay? Why? she wondered. Then she realized: Jesus came to show us how much God loved us by coming in an ordinary way—not as a King so great that we would be afraid of Him. Who could be afraid of a baby in a manger? She closed her eyes as she rocked and prayed, "Thank you, Jesus, for coming."

—⁂—

Finally. Away from the crowds. Alone as a family, even if this wasn't "home" and even though it smelled like animals instead of sweet baby's things. Joseph dipped a cup of fresh water for Mary to sip. She'd been so brave for one so young. And now he smiled as she soaked up her reward: a baby. A perfect baby. God resting His head against her arms, nuzzling close and heaving a tired little sigh. Could this be? Could this be true? He looked so human. But they knew this was no ordinary child.

"Mary," Joseph said, "tell me again what the angel told you."

Mary looked up at her husband and spoke, keeping her voice low so she wouldn't disturb the baby. "Gabriel said 'the Holy one to be born will be called the Son of God.'"

Joseph wrapped his arms around Mary and together they both gazed at Jesus. Mary touched one of her son's little fingers and watched it curl around her own. "Thank you, Jesus," she whispered, "for coming."

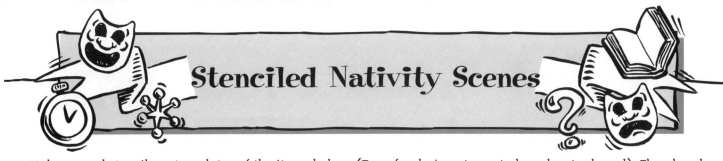

# Stenciled Nativity Scenes

Make several stencils or templates of the items below. (Transfer designs to posterboard or tagboard). Then hand each of the children a piece of manila paper and ask them to draw a large outline of a stable on it. Then put a pile of stencils or templates in the middle of the table and let them trace the outlines of the Nativity figures and fill in the details as they like. Play or sing Christmas carols, bring some cinnamon potpourri to fill the room with a Christmas smell. (If you have time and energy, you might even serve gingerbread cookies for a treat.)

# Thank You for Coming!

## Activity Sheet

### for Grades 1-3

Color pieces first. Then cut out each piece. Put a brad through Mary's arm and shoulder so that it can move up and down. Glue baby Jesus in her arms (behind her hand) — following dotted line. Put a little glue only on the top of Mary's head and put her head covering in place. If desired you may staple a loop of yarn or ribbon to the top of Mary and Baby to use as a Christmas ornament.

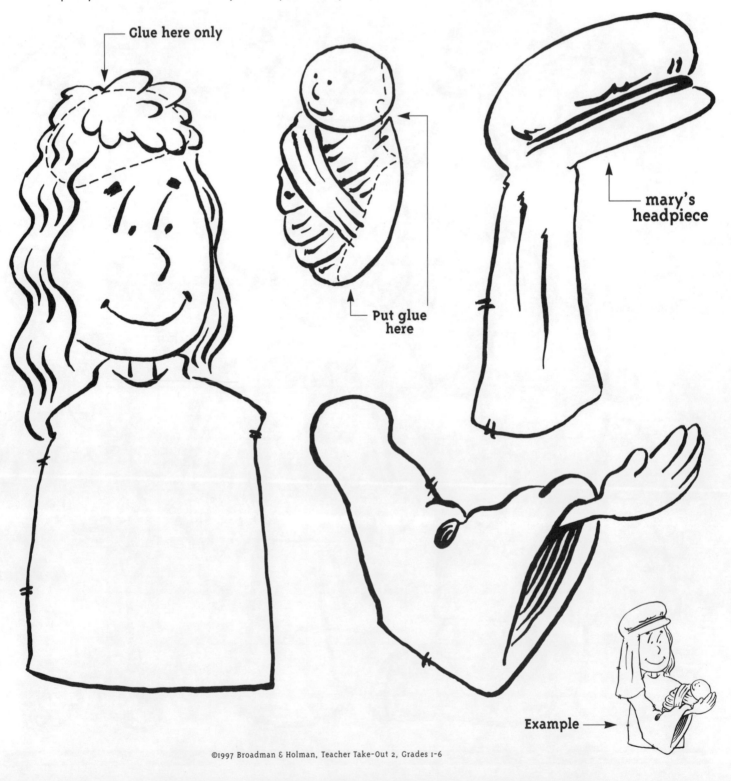

Glue here only

Put glue here

mary's headpiece

Example →

# Thank You for Coming!

## Activity Sheet

### for Grades 4-6

Look in the graph below for the following words from the Christmas story and circle them.

Joy To The World
From: Jesus

| M | O | I | Q | M | B | A | B | Y | B |
|---|---|---|---|---|---|---|---|---|---|
| M | A | N | T | J | P | O | T | C | I |
| M | A | N | G | O | E | S | P | H | R |
| C | N | R | G | S | A | S | N | R | T |
| V | G | X | Y | E | R | T | J | I | H |
| W | E | J | I | P | R | A | E | S | P |
| B | L | J | O | H | G | R | S | T | B |
| R | S | H | E | P | H | E | R | D | S |
| A | G | A | B | R | I | E | L | C | O |
| W | I | S | E | M | E | N | A | S | N |
| B | E | T | H | L | E | H | E | M | P |

**Baby**

**Joseph**

**Mary**

**Birth**

**Son**

**Christ**

**Gabriel**

**Wisemen**

**Bethlehem**

**Shepherds**

**Star**

**Angels**

**Manger**

# Good News!

*(based on Luke 2: 8-14)*

Maria let the tears fall on the hospital bed where her daughter, Rosita, lay ill, and asleep. She looks so small and weak. The doctors had been looking for someone who could donate a kidney to her little girl for months now. It would be the only way she could live. But someone had to be willing to go through surgery and give up one of their kidneys. But usually only relatives will do such a thing and none of Rosita's relatives had what the doctors called a "match" when they tested them. Since Rosita was adopted as a baby, it was even harder to find a match. If there wasn't a match, Rosita's body would not accept the kidney.

"Please, God," Maria prayed for the thousandth time," we need a miracle." In the distance Maria could hear carolers singing "Silent Night." She feel asleep, her head near her Rosita's pillow.

"Maria! Wake up! I've got GREAT NEWS! It's going to make you SO HAPPY!!"

Maria stirred and lifted a groggy head. Who was this speaking? An angel dressed in white? No. A nurse.

"Maria, listen, we've found a match. Your neighbor and friend, Melissa, is going to give up one of her kidneys for Rosita."

Maria began to weep with relief and happiness. Outside the hospital windows, sparkling snowflakes fell like diamonds to the ground, some church bells were playing "Joy to the World!"

"Yes!" said Maria as she put her hands together in prayer and looked toward the starry sky outside. "Joy to the World!" Now every Christmas Eve, Rosita and Maria and Melissa sing a special Christmas carol together, remembering the One who saved them all from sin, and thanking God for helping Melissa save Rosita's life. Can you guess what they sing?

*(Author note: This is based on a true story involving friends of mine.*
*And "Rosita" is still doing great! Joy to the World!)*

———ɯ———

In the soft light of the moon, Marcus reached down to pat a new baby lamb on the head. Its mother ba-a-a-ed. All was calm, all was quiet. For the moment.

Then suddenly the sky burst open and a brilliant light flooded the hills. Marcus dropped to his knees in fear.

Then an angel appeared and said, "Don't be afraid. I bring you good news of great joy! Today a Savior has been born to you. You'll find him lying in a manger."

What happened next left all the Shepherds kneeling on the ground with their eyes wide and mouths open. For a whole sky full of angels appeared with the one that had spoken and begin to praise God together saying, "Glory to God in the highest, and on earth peace to men!"

# Good News Message Chain

Write out the following phrases from the angels' messages on strips of paper at least 4 inches wide and 11 inches long. (You may use a piece of regular paper, cut in half lengthwise.) Have a big roll of tape handy. Turn over the strips of paper. Let each child pick one until they are all gone (if your class is small some children may get more than one.)

For grades 1-3, the teacher will need to read the message from Luke 2:10-12, 14 , one phrase at a time. The child with the corresponding phrase will come to the front and tape his message strip to the one before until you've made a looooong Scripture chain.

For grades 4-6, they are on their own. Have them work together to arrange the strips in correct order by reading the text from a Bible. (The following is from the New International Version. If you are using another translation, just copy the phrases from it.) After the chain is finished, have the class read the results aloud together.

Do not

be afraid.

I bring you

good news

of great joy

that will be

for all the people.

Today

in the town of David

a Savior

has been born

to you;

he is Christ

the Lord.

This will be

a sign to you:

You will find

a baby

wrapped in cloths

and lying

in a manger.

Glory to God

in the highest,

and on earth

peace to men

on whom

his favor rests.

# Good News!

## Activity Sheet

### for Grades 1-3

Someone was not paying attention at all when the teacher read today's Bible message and got completely mixed up! Would you help them get it right by marking out the wrong words and putting in the right ones?

There were leopards living out in the farm nearby, keeping a watch over their clocks by night. And an anthill of the Lord appeared to them and gravy shown around them, and they were brave. But the angel said to them, "Be so afraid. I bring you good shoes of great toy that will be for all the purple. Today in the town of Donald a Savior has been born; he is Christ the Lord. This will be a lime for you: You will find the baby wrapped in moths and lying in danger.

# Good News!

## Activity Sheet

### for Grades 4-6

Help fill in "The Sheepherder's Nightly" News Scroll. Draw a picture to go with the caption. Fill in the blanks to answer the journalistic questions. (Find clues in Luke 2:8-14.) When you are finished, carefully tear around the edges and to make it look old, rub a brown crayon on the torn edges. Roll up like a scroll and tie with a ribbon. You may want to use this as a Christmas decoration and share it with your family on Christmas Eve or Christmas morning.

# The Sheepherder's Nightly

**tear edges**

## "ANGELS LIGHT UP SKY ON SHEPHERD'S HILL"

Angels say they bring _____ _____ of _____ _____.

(For who?) _____

(When?) _____ (Where?) _____

(What happened?) _____

(Who is He?) _____

What sign should we look for? _____

**write out angels' praises in verse 14**

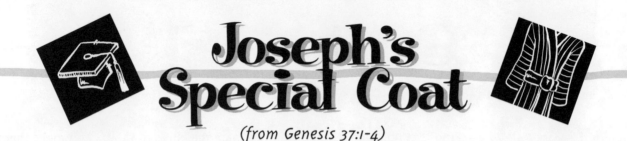

# Joseph's Special Coat

## (from Genesis 37:1-4)

Rachel watched from the football stands as her father escorted her big sister, Colyer, out to the field for the Homecoming Ceremonies. Colyer looked incredible: long ringlets of natural golden curls flowing down her back, her silky blue dress flowed gracefully with every step. Her big blue eyes and bright smile flashed charm, even from such a distance. Rachel couldn't help noticing the look of pride in her dad's eyes as he patted Colyer's arm.

"It's not fair! It's not fair!" cried Rachel inside. "She has everything! And now, I'm sure, they'll announce she's Homecoming Queen, too."

But Rachel was wrong. Another girl received the crown. Now Rachel's insides were really confused. Part of her was truly sad Colyer didn't win, because, she had to admit, Colyer was a good sister. Oh, they had their differences. But Colyer had always loved and stood up for Rachel.

The next day, Rachel and her mom were sipping colas outside on the porch swing when her mom asked, "Rachel, do you know how much Daddy and I love you and how proud we are of you?"

"Yeah, I guess so," Rachel said quietly.

"You know Colyer goes off to college in four months, and it may seem like she's been getting more than her fair share of attention," Mom said. "It's just that we're going to miss her so much. Just like we'll miss you when you graduate in a few years." Mom tousled Rachel's hair. " I'm so glad you're going to hang around here a little longer. You're a little Sunshine Kid, ya know that?"

Suddenly Rachel felt a tear slide down her cheek. She said, "I'm going to miss Colyer, too." And to her relief, she found she really meant it.

—⋙—

Israel couldn't wait to give Joseph the beautiful new coat he'd had made especially for him. Joseph was growing up so fast, already he was seventeen! "Oh, how his birth made this old man happy," Israel thought. "He's grown up just like his mother. Smart, good-looking, charming and He loves our God.

Joseph loved his coat! But every time Joseph's brothers saw it, they realized their father loved Joseph more than them. And because Israel didn't love his other sons as much, they grew to hate Joseph and couldn't say one nice thing to him. It would take lots of tears, lots of pain and lots of forgiveness. But one day, years from now, Joseph and his brothers would find out how much they really loved each other.

# What Makes You So Special?

Begin the class today by asking that question. Let the children share the kinds of things that make them special to their parents, their friends and to each other. Tell each one of the children something you like about them—something that makes them special to you.

Then ask, "Was it right for Israel to show more love to Joseph than to his other sons? Does our Father in heaven do that with us? No! Do you know how special each one of us is to our Heavenly Father?"

Draw a big heart on a chart with a marker or on a black board with chalk. Write, "That's how much He loves me" in the middle of it. Then read, one verse at a time, from Psalm 139: 13-16. After each verse, let a different child come up to the board and draw a line from the heart and write the following phrases out to the side. Then have them put a circle around what they wrote with different colored chalk or markers. Option: You may prefer to have the older children each draw their own diagram using pencils, colored markers or crayons on individual sheets of paper. When you finish it should look something like this:

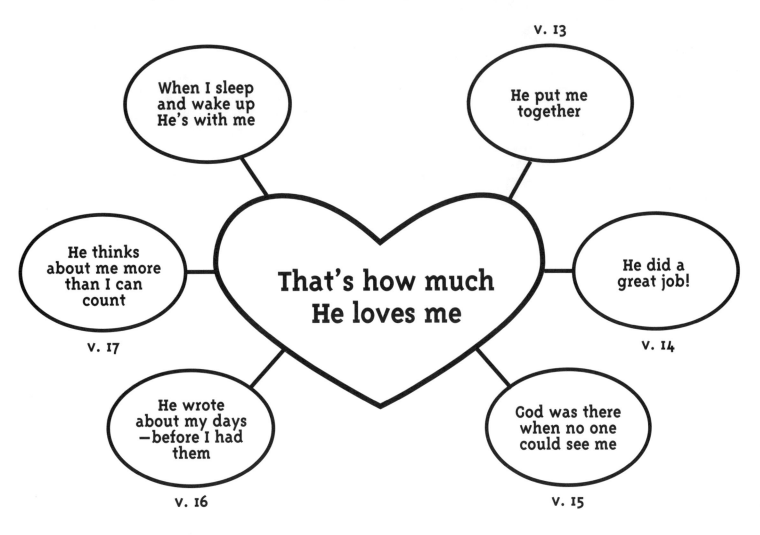

# Joseph's Special Coat
## Activity Sheet
### for Grades 1-3

Color Joseph. Then color his coat with as many different colors as you can find.
Cut around Joseph following the line. Cut out his coat and glue it on him.

cut along line →

← cut along line

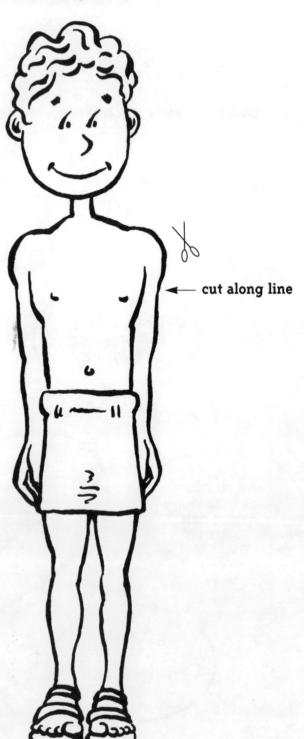

# Joseph's Special Coat
## Activity Sheet
### for Grades 4-6

Answer the questions below. Then cut along the solid line and fold the flaps inward,
as shown in the diagram until you have made the front of a coat. Decorate it like Joseph's robe.

## JOSEPH

**Why did Israel love Joseph so much?**

_____

_____

_____

_____

Genesis 37:3

**What did Joseph's father make him?**

_____

**How old was Joseph?**

_____

Genesis 37:1

**Were Joseph's brothers happy about Joseph's gift?**

_____

**Why or why not?**

_____

_____

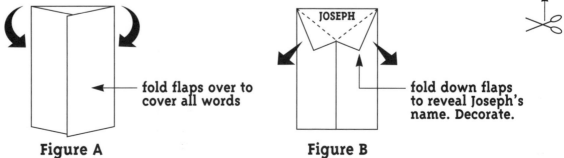

fold flaps over to cover all words

**Figure A**

JOSEPH

fold down flaps to reveal Joseph's name. Decorate.

**Figure B**

# Best Friends

*(based on 1 Sam. 18:1-4, 20:42)*

Michael had dreaded this day for months. Seeing the moving van in front of his best friend's house was too much! He watched out his bedroom window as movers carried Chad's bunkbed out the door.

Now Michael saw Chad's father carrying a set of fishing poles and setting them in the back of his pick-up. "What will I do without my fishing buddy now?"

Just then he heard a knock at the back door. Chad was standing there with his favorite fishing lure held out in his hand. "I want you to have this," he said, his voice trembling, "You're the best friend I've ever had."

Michael tried to talk but all that came out was gibberish and tears. He hated to cry, but this time he couldn't help it. He had to admit, he loved his friend. They gave each other a bear hug and promised to write. But, today, it hurt. It always hurts to say "good-bye" to your very best friend in the world.

—✺—

The first time Jonathan met David he knew they were meant to be friends. Jonathan loved David as much as he loved himself.

Now they were sharing one of the saddest days either of them had known. For Jonathan's father, King Saul, was jealous of David because David was a mighty warrior and the people of Israel loved him more than Saul.

Today, Jonathan had to tell David some horrible news. His father was going to try to kill David. To protect himself, David would have to leave and stay hidden for a long time. On this, their last meeting, they held each other and wept. And David, who'd come to love Jonathan, too, wept the most.

## Friends Can!

Reproduce and cut out the following questions into strips and put them in a coffee can that has been covered with paper and labeled "Friends Can!" Let each child pick a question to answer about friendship. (Put the questions back in the can for re-use if you have more than 10 in the class.)

1. What's the best thing about your friend?

2. What's the most fun thing you like to do together?

3. How do you show your friends that you care when they are feeling sad?

4. What's the funniest thing that ever happened to you and one of your friends?

5. Tell about the first time you met one of your best friends.

6. What cartoon or TV character does your friend remind you of?

7. What's one of the nicest things a friend has ever done for you?

8. Did you and your friend ever have a fight? How did you make up?

9. Do you usually go first and pick out what to do, or does your friend? How do you work that out?

10. If you met someone without a friend how could you help them not feel lonely?

# Best Friends
## Activity Sheet
### for Grades 1-3

Draw a picture and fill in the blanks of each caption in the Friendship Album below.
When you are finished, cut out album and fold along dashed line.
Write "Friends Can" on the front and decorate like an album cover.

## Me and My Friends

This is me and my friend _____
playing _____ .

This is my friend _____
with (his or her) favorite toy.

Here's my friend _____
eating _____ .

This is my friend _____
in front of _____ .

# Best Friends
## Activity Sheet
### for Grades 4-6

Fill in the blanks below and you will have a story to keep and share.

## The Story of a Friendship

My friend _____ and I met when we were _____ years old. _____(friend's name) has _____ hair, _____ eyes and wears _____ a lot.

The thing I liked most about my new friend is that _____ _____ .

We like to play _____ and talk about _____ .

When I'm sad, _____ (friend's name) makes me feel better by _____ .

Once we got to go to _____ together. It was really _____ . We saw _____ and _____ . I'll never forget that day!

My friend has _____ brothers and _____ sisters. Their names are _____ .

_____ (he or she) lives _____ .

I thank God for giving me a friend like _____ .

(Draw a picture of you and your friend on the other side)